ESL ANIMALS 2
The ALPHABET   M TO Z

Student Reader
Student Workbook
Teacher Guide

Learning English Curriculum
Copyright © 2023 Learning English Curriculum. ALL RIGHTS RESERVED.

You are permitted to print or photocopy as many copies as you need for your school.

Online distribution is not permitted. Please contact us if you wish to teach online.

Re-Sales is not permitted.

Notice: Learning English Curriculum makes every reasonable effort to obtain from reliable sources accurate, complete, and timely information about the tests covered in this book. Nevertheless, changes can be made in the tests or the administration of the tests at any time and Learning English Curriculum makes no representation or warranty, either expressed or implied as to the accuracy, timeliness, or completeness of the information contained in this book. Learning English Curriculum make no representations or warranties of any kind, express or implied, about the completeness, accuracy, reliability, suitability or availability with respect to the information contained in this document for any purpose. Any reliance you place on such information is therefore strictly at your own risk.

The author(s) shall not be liable for any loss incurred as a consequence of the use and application, directly or indirectly, of any information presented in this work. Sold with the understanding, the author is not engaged in rendering professional services or advice. If advice or expert assistance is required, the services of a competent professional should be sought.

Published by:
Learning English Curriculum

ISBN: 9781772454062

Visit us online:
https://www.efl-esl.com

ESL ANIMALS 2
M TO Z

STUDENT READER

This Student Reader is Ready to Use.

It is Part of the Colorful Conversational Series that Includes
a Student Reader, Workbook,
and a Teacher's Guide with Unit Tests and a Final Test.

In this Reader the children listen, identify beginning sounds from M to Z, read and role-play the dialogues, and suggest what they would do if they were meeting the animals with the storybook characters.

Teacher instructions are provided in small boxes on each page.

George and Daisy Stocker

E-mail: **info@efl-esl.com**

ALPHABET ANIMALS FROM M TO Z

STUDENT READER

	CONTENTS		PAGES
Introduction			28
Chapter 13	Mm	Adventure Park	29 -31
Chapter 14	Nn	Narwhales	32 - 33
Chapter 15	Oo	Octopus	34 - 36
Chapter 16	Pp	Porcupines / Porpoises	37 - 39
Chapter 17	Qq	Quokkas	40
Chapter 18	Rr	Reindeer	41 - 42
Chapter 19	Ss	Squirrels	43
Chapter 20	Tt	Tiger / Turtles	44 - 46
Chapter 21	Uu	Umbrellabird	47 - 48
Chapter 22	Vv	Vultures	49
Chapter 23	Ww	Walrus / Western Gorillas	50 - 51
Chapter 24	Xx	X-ray Tetra	52
Chapter 25	Yy	Yaks	53 - 54
Chapter 26	Zz	Zebra	55

CHAPTERS 13 to 26

ESL Animals is presented in a graphics novel format stressing listening, speaking, understanding, writing and phonics. It introduces the alphabet letters from M to Z and associates them with animals, birds and food. Numbers from 13 to 22 are included. It is designed for children aged 6 to 8 years who have matured past the need for reading readiness and fine motor control practice. Graphics are used to demonstrate the meaning of the text.

The **Student Reader** can be used by many different classes as the children don't write in it. Teacher instructions are given in smaller print at the bottom of each page. The suggestions provide oral practice and enhance student understanding. They also provide references with page numbers for the Workbook and Guide. **Example: Workbook:** Page _ **Guide**: Picture Bingo Page _ **Tests** Page _

This Reader introduces the alphabet from M to Z with pictures and simple dialogue for role-plays that are to be read from left to right. The children are introduced to their teacher, Polly Parrot. He explains the names and sounds of the letters, using key words and pictures. The two storybook characters, George and Elizabeth, introduce themselves. They speak to the children in your class saying, "Come with us. It'll be a blast!" At the end of each chapter George and Elizabeth introduce the next lesson by talking about what they are going to do next.

The **Workbook**
Polly Parrot, the teacher, names the letters and models what they say and gives instructions. The children have practice printing the letters, key words and question answers between the lines. Understanding of the key words is reinforced with colorful pictures. The exercises become increasingly difficult. Where the exercise provides more than one line for printing, it is for the teacher to decide how many times the children print the sentence.

The numbers are introduced with oral counting of a series of pictures.
Teacher suggestions are provided in small print on each page. These guide the teacher in presenting the lessons in the best way.

The **Teacher's Guide** includes **Tests** to be given after every fourth lesson and **Picture Bingo** games that review and reinforce the children's understanding of the materials taught. These are very important as they motivate the children to attend and understand.

Call the **Teacher's Captions** first. **Play the game many times until the children are successful.** When the students are ready, call the **Enrichment Captions**. These captions contain new vocabulary but are designed to teach the children to use context clues to find the correct picture.

CHAPTER 13

Read: George and Elizabeth's dialogue from left to right several times. Point to the sign. Have the children read the sign.
Explain new vocabulary as needed.

Ask: What is the boy's name? (His name is George.)   Ask: What is the girl's name? (Her name is Elizabeth.)
Ask: Do you have a sister? (Yes, I do. / No, I don't.)   Ask: Do you have a brother? (Yes, I do. / No, I don't.)

CHAPTER 13 CONTINUED

Explain that the children are at the Play Park. Have the students point to the **Monkey School**.
Read the dialogue from left to right several times. The children will use the context and pictures to understand new words.

Divide the class in half. Have the two groups role-play the dialogue for George and Elizabeth. Change roles many times.

Ask: Where are George and Elizabeth? *(They are at the Play Park.)*

Ask: What does Elizabeth see? *(She sees the Monkey School.)*

Ask individual students: What do you think monkeys do at school? *(I think…)*

Ask: What does Elizabeth think they do? *(She thinks they learn to climb trees.)*

Ask: What do you think the children are going to do? *(They're going to look inside the monkey school.)*

WORKBOOK: Page 33

Student Reader

CHAPTER 13 CONTINUED

Explain: The children are looking inside the Monkey School.
Read the green board and the dialogue orally. **Role-play as explained on page 30.**

Ask: Does the Monkey School look like your school? *(Yes, it does.) (No, it doesn't.)*

Ask: What letter are the Monkeys learning? *(They're learning Mm)*

WORKBOOK: Page 34

Student Reader

CHAPTER 14

This is **Nn**

Narwhales live in the cold water.
They talk to their friends with their long tusks.

Do they get cold?

No, they don't get cold.

I'd get cold!

I'd like to talk with a long tusk!

Information: Narwhales have sensory nerves at the end of their tusks for communication. **Explain:** The narwhales don't get cold because their blood is cold. We would get cold because our blood is warm. **Role-play. See Page 30**.

Ask: Do narwhales live in cold water? *(Yes, they live in cold water.)* **Ask:** Do narwhales get cold? *(No, they don't.)*

Ask: Would we get cold? *(Yes, we'd get cold.)* **Ask:** Do we have warm blood? *(Yes, we have warm blood.)*

Ask: Would you like to have tusks? *(Yes, I/We would.)* Can narwhales talk with their tusks? *(Yes, they can.)*

WORKBOOK: page 35

Student Reader

CHAPTER 14 CONTINUED

Narwhales hunt for fish under the ice.

I wonder what they're talking about?

Maybe they're talking about fish.

Let's see the octopus

Read the dialogue orally several times. Have the children read with you.

Say: Point to the sea ice. **Role-play. See Page 30. Ask:** What do narwhales eat? *(They eat fish.)*

Ask: What do narwhales do under the ice? *(They hunt for fish.)*

Ask: Do narwhales talk to their friends? *(Yes, they do.)*

Ask: Do they talk with their tusks? *(Yes, they do.)*

Ask: Do you eat fish? *(Yes, I/We do.) (No, I/We don't.)*

WORKBOOK: Page 36

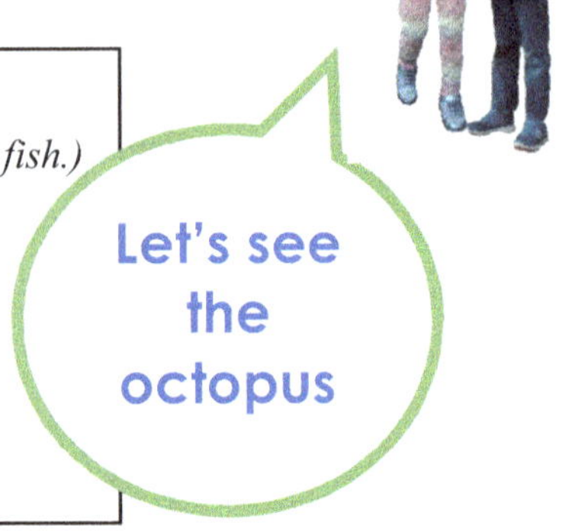

Student Reader

CHAPTER 15

Read the dialogue to the class. Have them read it with you several times.   **Role-play** three or four times.
Ask: How many octopus are in the picture? *(There are 3 octopus.)*   **Ask:** How many fish are there? *(There are 10 fish.)*
Ask: Where do octopus live? *(They live in the ocean.)*   **Ask:** What do octopus eat? *(They eat shellfish.)*

WORKBOOK: Page 37

Student Reader

CHAPTER 15 CONTINUED

Read what Elizabeth is thinking. Explain that she doesn't say it out-loud. Have the children point to all the shells on the page.

Read the dialogue with the students.   Role-play several times.

Say: Point to the shell with the hole.   Ask: What sea creature made the hole? *(An octopus made the hole.)*

Ask: Why did it make the hole? *(It wanted to have something to eat.)*   Ask: What does Elizabeth want? *(She wants some shells.)*

Ask: Does Elizabeth want something to eat? *(No, she doesn't)*   Ask: Would you like to have some shells? *(Yes, I would. / (No, I wouldn't.)*

Ask: What is the biggest octopus doing? *(It's making a hole in the shell.)*

Ask: What will the octopus do with the sea creature inside? *(It will eat it.)*

WORKBOOK: Page 38   **TEACHER'S GUIDE:** Picture Bingo 5 - Pages 136-163

Student Reader

CHAPTER 15 CONTINUED

"What's that octopus doing?"

"Is it trying to open the jar?"

"Look! It opened it!"

"I think octopus are smart."

"The porcupines are next."

Information: Octopus are problem solving creatures. **Read** the dialogue and role-play.

Ask: What did the octopus do? *(It opened the jar.)* **Discuss.**

GUIDE: Continue Picture Bingo

CHAPTER 16

This is **Pp**

Porcupines live near the trees. They have thousands of sharp quills.

Their sharp quills keep them safe.

We're scaring them! We'll see the porpoises tomorrow.

Information: Porcupines are covered with as many as 30,000 quills that are about 15 centimeters long. The quills stand up when the porcupine is scared. **Read, point to and say Pp**. Have the children listen to the first sound and say "porcupine" **Read** what Polly Parrot says and have the students read with you.

Say: Point to the porcupines on the ground. **Ask:** How many porcupines are on the ground? (There are 2 on the ground.)

Ask: How many are climbing a tree? (One porcupine is climbing a tree.)

Ask: What protects the porcupines? (Their sharp quills protect the porcupines.) **Repeat** the questions many times.

WORKBOOK: Page 39   TEACHER'S GUIDE: Continue with Picture Bingo

Student Reader

CHAPTER 16 CONTINUED

Porpoises live in the ocean. They come to the surface of the water to breathe.

The porpoises are following the boat!

Look behind you! A baby porpoise is jumping with its mother.

Let's ask Dad if we can go out in a boat.

Information: Porpoises are the same family as dolphins but their teeth and jaws are different. They eat small fish. They are seen in groups and are known to follow boats at sea.

Read and explain what Polly Parrot is saying and have the students read it with you several times.

Ask: Where do porpoises live? (They live in the ocean.)

Ask: Why do the porpoises come to the surface? (They need to breathe.)   **Ask:** Do you breathe? (Yes, I/We breathe.)

Have the children read the dialogue and **Role-play it** many times.

WORKBOOK: Page 40-41   TEACHER'S GUIDE Continue with Picture Bingo

Student Reader

CHAPTER 16 CONTINUED

We're lucky today!

I want to see the baby porpoise.

They can jump so high! I'm going to learn to jump high in the water.

Thanks for bringing us, Dad.

Let's see the quokkas tomorrow!

Read the dialogue to the children and have them read it with you several times.
Role-play in the large group and in small groups, having the students change roles.

Ask: Are the kids lucky today? (Yes, they're lucky today.)   **Ask:** Why are they lucky? (They're seeing the porpoises)

Ask: What does Elizabeth want to see? (She wants to see a baby porpoise.)

Ask: Can the porpoises jump high? (Yes, they can jump high.)

Ask: What does George want to learn to do? (He wants to learn to jump high in the water.)

Ask: Who says "Thanks" to Dad? (George says "Thanks" to his Dad)

TEACHER'S GUIDE: TEST 5 - Pages 124 - 127

Student Reader

CHAPTER 17

This letter is

 This quokka lives in a hot dry place.

I wish the baby would come out.

It looks like it's comfortable in there.

Let's see the reindeer.

Okay!

Information: the quokkas are small marsupials about 40 to 45 centimeters long. They live in Australia and on the nearby islands. They look like a small kangaroo but they can climb small trees. The baby lives in its mother's pouch until it's about six months old. They eat plants and seeds.

Read what Polly Parrot is saying and role-play the dialogue.   **Say:** Point to the mother quokka / baby quokka.

Ask: Where is the baby quokka? *(It's in its mother's pouch.)*   **Ask:** Do you think it's comfortable? *(Yes, I think it's comfortable.)*

WORKBOOK: Pages 42-43   Continue with Picture Bingo 5 as needed.

Student Reader

CHAPTER 18

Rr Reindeer live in the north in the summer. They eat the grass that grows in the wet ground.

Here are the reindeer!

Wow! Look at his antlers!

Information: Reindeer live in large herds on the Arctic Tundra of North America, Europe and Asia.

Read what Polly Parrot says several times. Have the children read it with you and explain the new vocabulary.

Role-play what Elizabeth and George say.   **Ask**: Where do the reindeer live? *(They live in the north.)*

Say: Point to the reindeer's antlers. The mother reindeer has a calf. Point to the calf.

Ask: What do they eat? *(They eat grass and branches.)*   **Ask**: Is the ground wet in summer? *(Yes, it is.)*

WORKBOOK: Page 44   Continue with Picture Bingo 5 as needed.

Student Reader

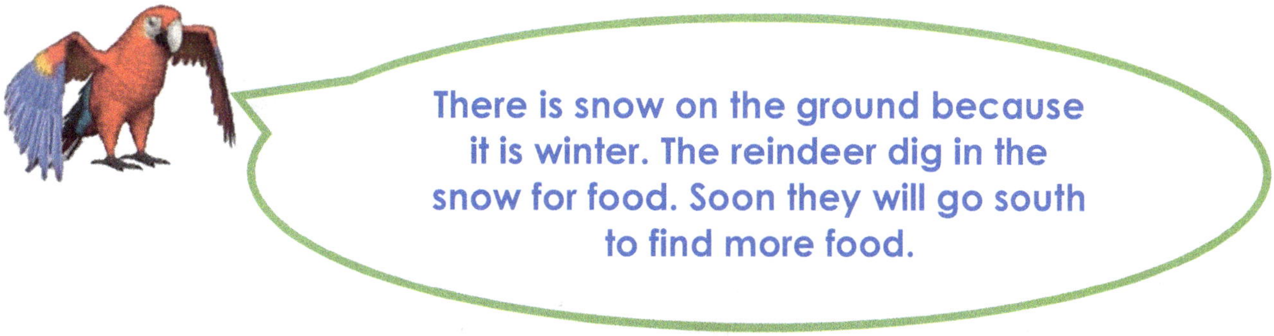

CHAPTER 18 CONTINUED

There is snow on the ground because it is winter. The reindeer dig in the snow for food. Soon they will go south to find more food.

I love the snow!

I don't want to dig for my food!

Maybe we can see the rabbits tomorrow.

Information: Reindeer travel farther than any land animal, some running as fast as 70 kilometers an hour. Their hooves adapt to the season. In summer when the tundra is soft and wet their footpads get bigger and become sponge-like. In winter their footpads shrink and harden to keep them from slipping in the hard crust of the snow.
They have two layers of fur to keep them warm.

Read what Polly Parrot says several times. Have the children read it with you and explain the new vocabulary.

Ask: Do we have snow in winter? *(Yes, we have snow in winter. / No, we don't have any snow in winter.)*

Ask: Do we dig food from the ground? *(Yes, we dig food from the ground.)* (ie carrots, beets, turnips etc.)

WORKBOOK: Page 45   **TEACHER'S GUIDE:** Picture Bingo 6 - Pages: 164 - 190

Student Reader

CHAPTER 19

Squirrels eat nuts and berries. They hide food in the forest in the fall and go to sleep for the winter.

Wow! It's hard to get through this tall grass.

Hey George, here's a squirrel!

I see its big furry tail. It's going to run away!

It's scared of me!

Let's see the tigers.

Read what Polly Parrot says. Have the students read with you several times, pointing to the nuts and berries as they read.
Have the class read the dialogue orally. **Role-play**, changing roles several times.

Ask: Why is it hard for George to walk? *(The grass is tall.)*   **Ask:** What does Elizabeth see? *(She sees a squirrel.)*

Ask: Where are George and Elizabeth? *(They are in the forest.)*   **Ask:** Can squirrels climb trees? *(Yes, they can.)*

WORKBOOK: Page 46   TEACHER'S GUIDE: Picture Bingo 6

CHAPTER 20

Tt is the first letter in tiger

**Some tigers live in cold snowy countries.
Other tigers live in hot countries.**

Their fur keeps them warm in the cold winter snow.

It must be hot in the jungle. I wonder what they eat?

Information: The tiger is the biggest, 2.5 meters long, and the most powerful of all the cats.
Have the students read what Polly Parrot is saying. **Role-play** several times.

Ask: Do we live in a cold place? *(Yes, we live in a colds place.) (No, we don't live...)*
(We are hot in summer and cold in winter)

Ask: Do we live in a hot place? *(Yes, we do.) No, we don't.) (In summer we are hot and...)*

WORKBOOK: Page 47   TEACHER'S GUIDE: Picture Bingo 6

CHAPTER 20 CONTINUED

Tigers are very dangerous animals! They hunt and eat crocodiles, snakes, rats, deer, and camels.

He's ferocious!

He's awesome!

Have the class read what Polly Parrot is saying and point to the animals as they read.

Explain that "**ferocious**" means violent, dangerous or not friendly. **Demonstrate.**
Awesome in this case means fearsome or overwhelming. **Demonstrate.**

Ask: What do tigers eat? (*They eat crocodiles, snakes, deer or camels.*)   **Role-play.**

WORKBOOK: Page 48   TEACHER'S GUIDE: Picture Bingo 6

Student Reader

CHAPTER 20 CONTINUED

Sea Turtles  live in the sea. They eat fish,  crabs  and jellyfish.

Would it eat me?

Polly Parrot says they eat fish, crabs and jellyfish.

I want to see the umbrellabird tomorrow.

Me too!

Information: This page reviews letters **Ss** and **Tt**.
Read Polly Parrot's message with the children. Have them point to the sea creatures in the message and say their names. (fish, crabs, jellyfish). **Read** the dialogue and **Role-play**

Ask: Would the sea turtle eat Elizabeth? *(No, it wouldn't.)* **Ask:** Are sea turtles dangerous? *(No, they aren't.)*

Ask: What do sea turtles eat? *(They eat fish, crabs and jellyfish.)* **Ask:** Do jellyfish live in the sea? *(Yes, they do.)*

Ask: Do you eat fish? *(Yes, I do. / No, I don't.)*

WORKBOOK: Page 49   **TEACHER'S GUIDE:** Picture Bingo 6

Student Reader

CHAPTER 21

U u is the first letter in **umbrellabird**.
The umbrellabirds live in the trees of the tropical jungle.
They hold onto the branches with their strong toes.

What's hanging down from its neck?

I don't know! Let's ask Mom.

Information: The umbrellabird lives in the rainforests of Central America. It has an umbrella like crest on its head and a long inflatable pouch on its throat. This pouch or wattle amplifies its loud booming call.

Read what Polly Parrot is saying, explaining "tropical jungle".

Have the children point to their neck, toes.   **Role-play** the dialogue several times.

Ask: *Is it hot in the jungle? (Yes, it is.)*   **Ask:** *Do you have toes? (Yes, I/We have toes.)*

WORKBOOK: Page 50   TEACHER'S GUIDE: Picture Bingo 6

Student Reader

47

CHAPTER 21 CONTINUED

Did you ask Mom?

Yes, she said the umbrellabird makes its pouch go BOOOOM BOOOOM to call its friends.

Wow! That's cool!

It's got an umbrella but I've got a hat.

Dad saw vultures in the park. Let's go!

Explain that the umbrellabird is named for the crest over its head that looks like an umbrella.
Ask: Do you have an umbrella? *(Yes, I have an umbrella.) (No, I don't have an umbrella.)*
Ask: How does the umbrellabird call its friends? *(It says, "BOOOOM!)*
Ask: What does Elizabeth have on her head? *(She has a hat.)*
Ask: Where does the umbrellabird live? *(It lives in the tropical jungle.)*
Ask: Where do you live? *(I /We live ...)*
   WORKBOOK: Page 51 - 52   **TEACHER'S GUIDE:** Picture Bingo 6

CHAPTER 22

V v is the first letter in vulture.

Where's he going?

Dad says vultures are scavengers. Maybe he's hunting for a dead animal.

Information: Vultures live in most countries, but not Australia/New Zealand. They are great scavengers. They keep the land clean by eating dead animals. **Introduce Vv**. **Role-play**.

Ask: What do vultures eat? (They eat dead animals.) **Ask:** Are vultures scavengers? *(Yes, they are.)* *(Yes, they are scavengers.)*

WORKBOOK: Page 53   **TEACHER'S GUIDE:** Picture Bingo 6

Student Reader

CHAPTER 23

W w is the first letter in walrus. Walruses live on the ice of the water of the Arctic Ocean. They eat clams  , snails , and fish.

The walruses don't look friendly!

Those mountains are scary!

Let's see the Western Gorillas.

Introduce what Polly Parrot says. **Role-play**

Ask: Is the water cold? (*Yes, it is.*) (*Yes, the water is cold.*)

Ask: Do you think the mountains are scary?
(*Yes, I think they are scary) No, I don't…*)

WORKBOOK: Page 54 **TEACHER'S GUIDE:** Picture Bingo 6

Student Reader

CHAPTER 23 CONTINUED

Western Gorillas are very big and strong.
They live in the hot jungles of Africa.
They eat leaves.

"I bet he could fight!"

"He's looking at me! He is scary!"

Introduce what Polly Parrot says. **Role-play.**

Ask: Is it hot in the Jungle? *(Yes, it's hot in the jungle)* *(Yes, it's hot.)*

Ask: Is the gorilla strong? *(Yes, he's strong.)* **Ask:** Are you strong? *(Yes, I'm strong.)* *(No, I'm not strong.)*

Ask: Would you be scared? *(No, I wouldn't be scared.)* *(Yes, I'd be scared.)*

WORKBOOK: Page 55   **TEACHER'S GUIDE:** Picture Bingo 6

CHAPTER 24

Xx Is the first letter in X-Ray Tetra.

The X-Ray Tetra are small fish that live in warm tropical rivers. They swim in groups called schools.

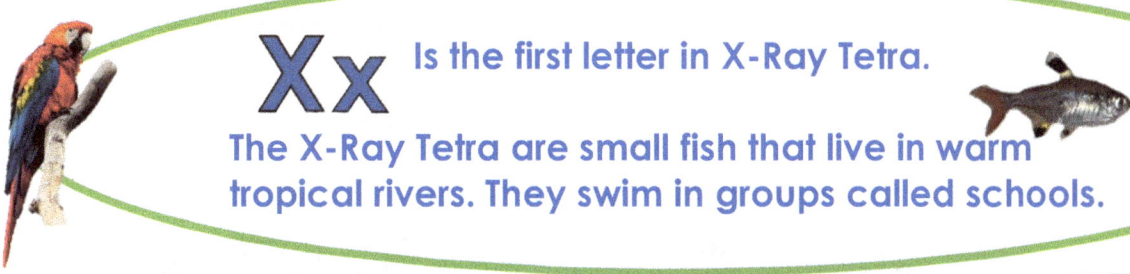

They're shiny!

I'd be cool to catch one! I love fishing.

Mom says we can see the Yaks.

Okay, let's go!

Explain: These small fish are named for their translucent skins that you can see through like an X ray.

Say: A group of fish is called a "school of fish". **Ask:** What is a group of fish called? *(It's called a school of fish.)*

WORKBOOK: Page 56   TEACHER'S GUIDE: Picture Bingo 6

Student Reader

CHAPTER 25

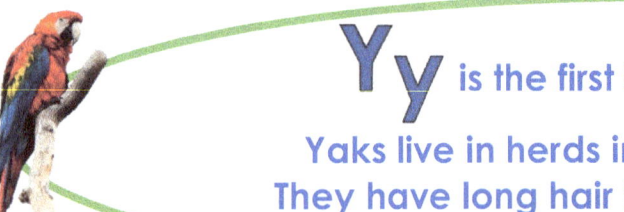

Yy is the first letter in Yak.

Yaks live in herds in the cold mountains.
They have long hair that keeps them warm.

It'd be cool to ride on one!

Wow! That would be a blast!

Let's ask Mom!

Information: Yaks live in the northern mountains of Asia. They supply the people with food and warm clothes. They feed on the mountain grass and use their horns to dig in the snow.
Have the students go to the **Workbook** for follow-up.

Have the children read what Polly Parrot says and **Role-play** the dialogue.

Ask: Would you want to ride on a yak? *(Yes, I would.) (No, I wouldn't)*

Ask: Do you think their horns are dangerous? *(Yes, I do!) (No, I don't think so.)*

  WORKBOOK: Page 57   **TEACHER'S GUIDE:** Introduce Picture Bingo 7 Pages 191 -217
NOTE: Letters Y and Z will be new.

Student Reader

CHAPTER 25 CONTINUED

Explain: George and Elizabeth's mother has taken them to a park where they can ride on the yaks. **Role-play.**

Ask: What is George sitting on? *(He's sitting on a yak.)*

Ask: What does George want the yak to do? *(He wants it to run.)*

Ask: What can Elizabeth do? *(She can climb onto the yak.) (She can climb into the saddle.) (She can climb up.)*

Ask: Does Elizabeth's yak have a saddle? *(Yes, it does.)*   **Ask:** Does George's yak have a saddle? *(No, it doesn't.)*

WORKBOOK: Page 58   TEACHER'S GUIDE: Picture Bingo 7

Student Reader

CHAPTER 26

Z z is the first letter in zebra.

Those zebras look like horses but they have stripes.

I wish we could ride them. The yaks were fun, yesterday!

Information: Zebras live on the African savannah. The exact placement of their black and white stripes is unique to each animal.

Have the students read what Polly Parrot says. **Role-play.**

Ask: Do the zebras have stripes? *(Yes, they have stripes.)*

WORKBOOK: Page 59   **TEACHER'S GUIDE:** Picture Bingo 7
WORKBOOK: Continue with Pages 60-63
TEACHER'S GUIDE: Picture Bingo 7 - **FINAL TEST:** Pages 132-135

Student Reader

ESL ANIMALS 2
The ALPHABET   M TO Z

Student Workbook

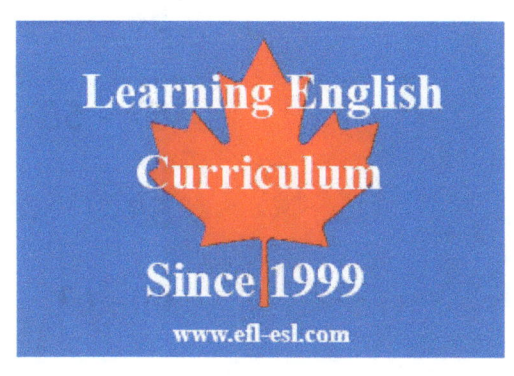

Daisy A. Stocker M.Ed.
George A. Stocker D.D.S.

ALPHABET ANIMALS FROM M TO Z
WORKBOOK
CONTENTS   PAGES

Introduction			32
Chapter 13	Mm	Monkey / numbers to 13	33 - 34
Chapter 14	Nn	Narwhales / numbers to 14	35 - 36
Chapter 15	Oo	Octopus / numbers to 15	37 - 38
Chapter 16	Pp	Porcupines / Porpoises /to 16	39 - 41
Chapter 17	Qq	Quokkas / numbers to 17	42 - 43
Chapter 18	Rr	Reindeer / numbers to 18	44 - 45
Chapter 19	Ss	Squirrels / numbers to 19	46
Chapter 20	Tt	Tiger / Turtles / numbers to 20	47 - 49
Chapter 21	Uu	Umbrellabird / numbers to 21	50 - 52
Chapter 22	Vv	Vultures	53
Chapter 23	Ww	Walrus / Western Gorillas	54 - 55
Chapter 24	Xx	X-ray Tetra	56
Chapter 25	Yy	Yaks	57 - 58
Chapter 26	Zz	Zebra	59
Review activities			60 - 63

CHAPTER 13

Hello, I'm Polly Parrot. I'm your English teacher.

This is capital **M**

This is small **m**

1. M

2. Monkey

3. m

4. monkey

5. I am a baby monkey.

Point to Polly Parrot. **Explain** that she is the teacher. **Read** what Polly says several times.

Have the children point to capital **M**, small **m**, the **words** and the **sentence** and read them with you several times. They are to print the letters, words and sentence on the lines.

Ask: Is the baby monkey eating? (*Yes, it is eating.*)   **Ask:** What is the baby monkey eating? (*It's eating a banana.*)

Student Workbook

CHAPTER 13 CONTINUED

Monkeys live in warm forests.
They eat nuts and fruit.

This monkey has a banana.

This is **13**

Count the monkeys.
1 2 3 4 5 6 7 8 9 10
11 12 13

How many?
_____

Explain that the mother monkey and the baby are in the forest. The baby is eating a nut.
First, read what Polly Parrot says about what the monkeys eat. Then have them read it with you several times. **Role-play**
Ask: Do you eat nuts? (Yes, I/We do) (No, I/We don't.)   **Ask:** Do you eat bananas? (Yes, I/We do) (No, I/We don't.)
Next: point to number 13 at the top of the page. Have the children follow Polly's directions and print their answer.

Student Workbook

CHAPTER 14

This is capital N and small n.

Narwhale starts with Nn.

1. N

2. Narwhale

3. n

4. narwhale

5. Narwhales eat fish.

Instructions: Have the class point to the letters as they read orally what Polly Parrot says.

The children are to read each line and print the letters and words.   **Ask:** What do narwhales eat? *(They eat fish.)*

Read the sentence with the students. They are to print the sentence between the lines.

Student Workbook

CHAPTER 14 CONTINUED

This narwhale caught a fish.
It's having a delicious lunch!

Count the fish.

How many fish did you find?

1 2 3 4 5 6 7 8 9 10
11 12 13 14

Explain that the narwhale and the fish are swimming under the ice. **Point out** the other creatures living on the ocean floor.

Ask: What is in the narwhale's mouth? *(A fish in its mouth.)* **Have the class read orally**, what Polly Parrot is saying.

They are to count the fish and circle the number telling how many. **Ask individuals:** How many did you find? *(I found ...)*

Student Workbook

CHAPTER 15

This is Oo

1. O

2. Octopus

3. o

4. Octopus swim.

5. Octopus eat shellfish.

6. Do octopus eat shellfish?

7. Yes, octopus

Instructions: Have the class read orally what Polly Parrot says. Guide them through the reading and printing of the letters, word, sentences, questions and question answers.

Remind them that the words are in the question. Oral repetition of vocabulary is very important as that's how children learn.

Ask: Do octopus swim? *(Yes, they swim.)* **Ask:** What do octopus eat? *(They eat shellfish.)*

Student Workbook

CHAPTER 15 CONTINUED

This is

George and Elizabeth have some riddles.

Try them. Print your answers.

It lives in the cold ocean.
It has a long tusk.
It can talk to its friends.
What is it?

It's a
_____

It lives in the ocean.
It has many legs.
It eats shellfish.
It can open jars.
What is it?

It's a
_____

| lion | monkey | octopus | kitten | narwhale |

Count the seashells:

1 2 3 4 5 6 7 8 9 10
11 12 13 14 15

How many?
_____

Read Polly Parrot's information and instructions to the class. **Explain** that with riddles they need to guess the answer.

Have the children read the riddles independently or with the whole class. They are to choose the answer from the box and print the word on the line.
Numbers: Have the class read the numbers orally. They are to count the shells and print the number on the line.

Student Workbook

CHAPTER 16

This is **Pp**

This porcupine is eating.

This porcupine family is eating grass. They are very prickly!

1. P

2. Porcupine

3. Prickly porcupines eat grass.

4. Do porcupines eat grass?

5. Yes, they

The class points to the letter, reading what Polly Parrot says. They read and print the sentence, question, and answer.

Explain: "prickly".

Ask: Are porcupines prickly? *(Yes, they are.)*

Ask: Are you prickly? *(No, I'm / we're not prickly.)*

Ask: What do porcupines eat? *(They eat grass.)*

Student Workbook

CHAPTER 16 CONTINUED

Porpoises live in friendly pods in the ocean.
They eat fish.

1. p

2. porpoises

3. Porpoises like people.

4. They eat fish.

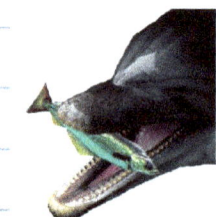

5. Do porpoises like people?

6. Yes,

7. Do porpoises eat fish?

8. Yes,

The children read what Polly Parrot says.   **Explain:** "pods" are like a group of friends or a family.   **Discuss.**
Have the students print the sentences and complete the answers. They'll find the words they need in the question.
Ask: Do porpoises eat people? *(No, they don't eat people.)*   **Ask:** Do porpoises eat fish? *(Yes, they eat fish.)*

Student Workbook

CHAPTER 16 CONTINUED

This is **16**

George and Elizabeth have more riddles.

Try them. Print your answers.

They live near the trees.
They have thousands of sharp quills that stand up when danger is near.
What are they?

They are
_____

These animals live in the ocean.
They swim to the surface to breathe.
They are friendly and like to follow boats.
What are they?

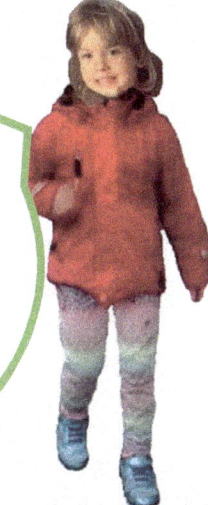

They are
_____

dogs
porcupines
octopus
porpoises
shellfish

Read Polly Parrot's information and instructions to the class. Have the children read the riddles independently or with the whole class. They are to choose the answer from the box and print the word on the line.
Instructions: The students are to make the picture show a total of **16 porpoises** swimming in the water.

Student Workbook

CHAPTER 17

This is **Qq** the first letter in quokka.

1. Q
2. q
3. Quokka
4. quokka
5. Quokkas hunt for food at night.
6. Do quokkas hunt at night?
7. Yes,
8. Do you hunt for food at night?
9. No, I don't

Have the class point to the letter as they read orally what Polly Parrot says. **They are to print** the letter, words, sentences, questions and complete the answers. **Note:** They'll find the words they need in the question except for the prepositions.

Ask: What is the quokka doing? *(It's hunting for food.)*

Ask: Do quokkas hunt for food at night? *(Yes, they hunt for food at night.)*

Student Workbook

CHAPTER 17 CONTINUED

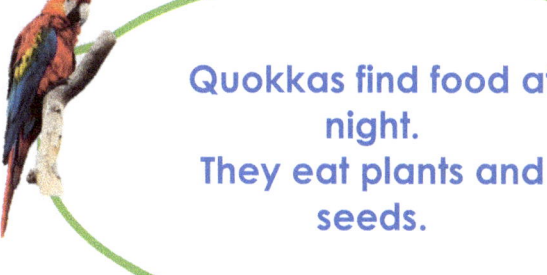

Quokkas find food at night.
They eat plants and seeds.

1. Do you eat plants?

2. Yes, I

Draw the plants that you eat.

17

Here are 10 seeds. Draw more seeds to make 17 seeds.

Read what Polly Parrot says and have the students read it with you.

Ask: Do you eat seeds? *(Yes, I/We eat seeds.)*   **Ask:** Do you eat plants? *(Yes, I / We eat plants)*

Instructions: Have the children read the question on the lines. They are to read and complete the answer. We suggest that they print the complete question and answer under the under the examples.

Point to 17. Have the students count to 17 orally.   **Print** the numbers on the board as necessary.

Say: Let's count the seeds in the picture. Have them read and follow the instructions above the picture.

Student Workbook

CHAPTER 18

Rr

Reindeer live in the cold snowy north.

1. R

2. Reindeer

3. r

4. reindeer

5. Do reindeer live in the north?

6. Yes, they

7. Is there snow on the ground?

8. Yes, there is

> Have the class point to the letter as they read orally what Polly Parrot says.
> They are to read each line and print the letters, words, sentences, questions and complete the question answers.
> **Discuss** the snowy north. **Explain** that it is very cold and snowy in the north for nine or ten months of the year.

Student Workbook

CHAPTER 18 CONTINUED

Let's count to 18.

1 2 3 4 5 6 7 8 9 10 11 12 13 14 15 16 17 18

18

There are 10 reindeer in the picture. Draw more reindeer to make the picture show 18 reindeer.

It's cold and snowy in the north.
Reindeer have two coats to keep them warm.

I have a winter coat and a summer coat.

Read the dialogue with the children. **Role-play.**   **Ask:** Is it cold in the north? *(Yes, it's cold in the north.)*
Ask: How many coats do reindeer have? *(They have two coats.)*
Ask: Does George have two coats? *(Yes, he does.)*   **Ask:** Is it warm in the north? *(No, it isn't.)*
Ask: Do you need a coat in winter? *(Yes, I do. / No, I don't.)*

Student Workbook

CHAPTER 19

Ss is the first letter in squirrel.
Squirrels eat nuts that they find in the forest.

1. S
2. s
3. Squirrel
4. squirrel
5. Do squirrels live in the forest?
6. Yes,
7. Do they sleep all winter?
8. Yes,

This squirrel has 1 nut. It needs 19 nuts. You draw 18 more nuts.

Have the class point to the letter as they read orally what Polly Parrot says.
They are to read and print each question. Then complete the answer.

Student Workbook

CHAPTER 20

 **T t** is the first letter in **tiger**.

1. T

2. t

3. Tiger

4. tiger

5. Are tigers dangerous animals?

6. Yes,

Crocodiles    **Reindeer**

7. What do tigers eat?

8. They eat

Have the students read what Polly Parrot says, **point** to the **Tt**, **point** to the Tiger and say "**tiger**".
They are to name the animals, read and print the questions, then complete printing the answers. **Print** "**and**" on the board.

Student Workbook

CHAPTER 20 CONTINUED

Can you guess this riddle?

It has four legs and big antlers.
It digs in the snow for food.
It eats grass.

It's a
_____

Can you guess?
This small animal lives in a hot dry place.
It eats seeds and plants.
The mother has her baby in a pouch.

It's a
_____

Choose your answers.

turtle   reindeer   porcupine   quokka   octopus

You feed the tiger more rats. It wants 20.

Read the riddles and the answers in the box with the class as appropriate.

Print 20 on the board and have the students count orally to 20. They are to fill the box with 20 quokkas

Student Workbook

CHAPTER 20 CONTINUED

The mother **sea turtle** lays her eggs in the sand.

The baby sea turtles dig themselves out of the sand and run into the sea.

They're all going into the water.

I wish I could hold one.

Information: This page is a review of **Ss** and **Tt**. Each year the sea turtles return to the beach where they were born, often swimming for long distances. The female turtle lays her eggs in the sand and returns to the sea. When the young hatch they dig their way out of the sand and run into the sea.

Read what Polly Parrot says with the class. **Introduce** the dialogue. **Role-play** several times.

Student Workbook

CHAPTER 21

The umbrellabird has its umbrella on its head.

You carry your umbrella when it rains.
Draw yourself holding the red umbrella
above your head.

Have the students read what Polly Parrot says and follow the instructions.

Ask: Do you have an umbrella? *(Yes, I do.) (No, I don't.)*

Ask: Is it raining in the picture? *(Yes. It's raining. or Yes, it is.)*

Student Workbook

CHAPTER 21 CONTINUED

U u is the first letter in umbrellabird.

1. U

2. u

3. Umbrellabird

4. umbrella

5. Does this bird say BOOOOM?

6. Yes,

7. Can you say BOOOM?

8. Yes,

9. It is an umbrella, isn't it?

10. Yes,

Read what Polly Parrot says. **Discuss** questions. **Number 10 answer**: (*Yes, it is.*)

Student Workbook

CHAPTER 21 CONTINUED

This is **21**

1. Count the umbrellabirds.
2. How many did you find?

I found _____.

Print the numbers from 1 to 21 on the umbrellas.

Read what Polly Parrot says and have the students follow the directions. **Explain:** Numbers 1 and 2 have been numbered.

Student Workbook

CHAPTER 22

**Vultures eat dead rats, mice, rabbits and fish.
They keep the land clean.**

1. V

2. V

3. Vultures

4. scavengers

5. Do vultures eat dead animals?

6. Yes, they

7. Do they eat dead rats?

8. Yes,

9. Are vultures scavengers?

10. Yes, they

Read what Polly Parrot says.   **Discuss** questions.   **Tell** the students to look in the questions for the words.

Student Workbook

CHAPTER 23

 **Ww** Walruses swim in the cold Arctic water.

1. W

2. W

3. walrus

4. water

5. Is the Arctic water cold?

6. Yes,

7. Do walruses swim in cold water?

8. Yes, they

9. Do you swim in cold water?

10. No, I don't

Read what Polly Parrot says. **Discuss** questions. **Tell** the students to look in the questions for the words.
Ask: Is there ice in the Arctic water? *(Yes, there is.) (Yes, there is ice in the Arctic water.)*

Student Workbook

CHAPTER 23 CONTINUED

This Western Gorilla has some nuts in his hand. He holds them between his thumb and fingers.

1. Does he have nuts in his hand?

2. Yes, he has

3. Do you have a thumb?

4. Yes, I

Say: Put your finger on your thumb. **Ask:** Do you have a thumb? *(Yes, I / We have a thumb.)*
Ask: Does a cat have a thumb? *(No, a cat doesn't have a thumb.)*

Student Workbook

CHAPTER 24

How many X-Ray Tetras are in this school?
Number the fish.
How many did you find?

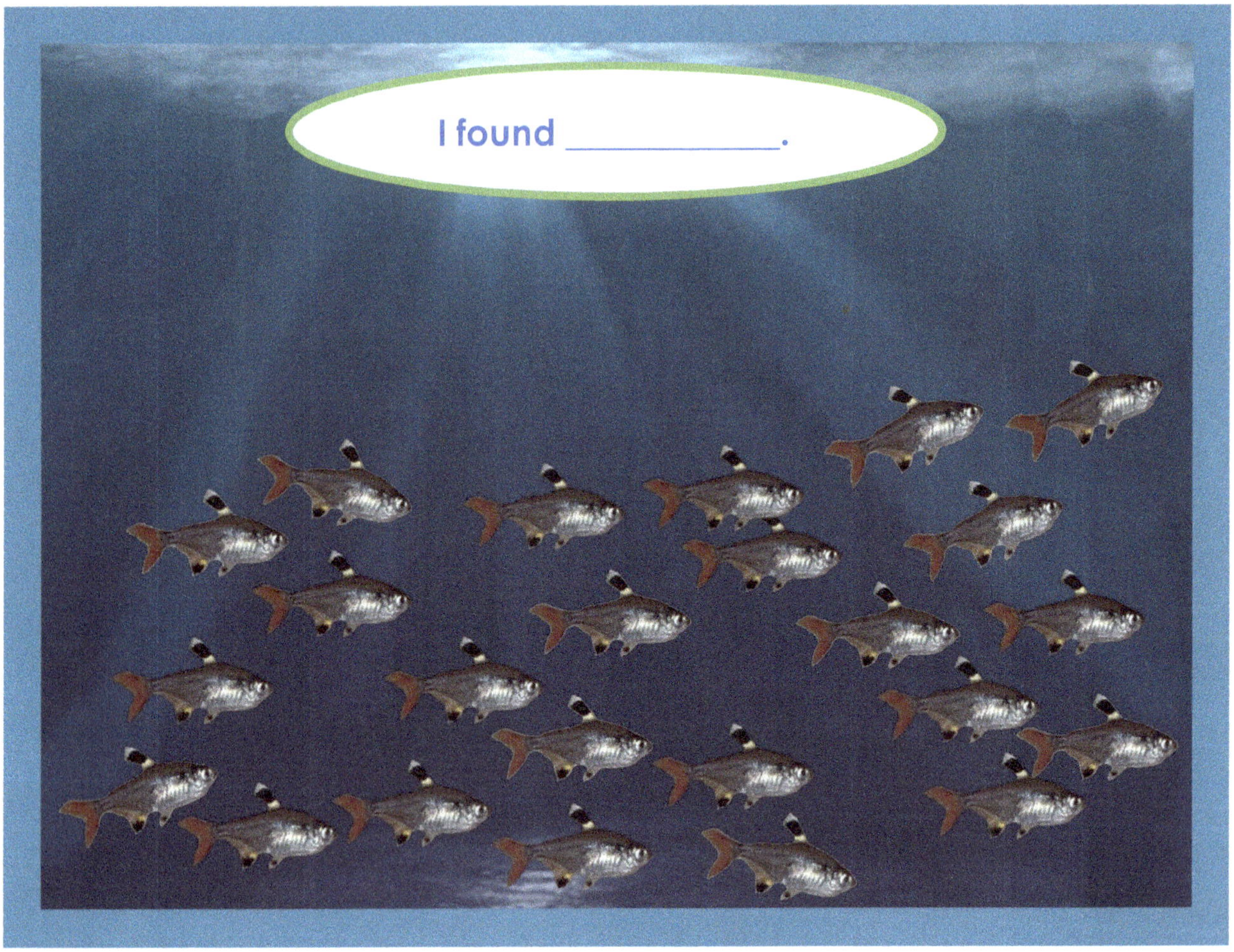

I found _____.

1. X

2. x

3. X-Ray Tetra

4. x-ray tetras

Instructions: Print the numbers on the board if necessary.

Student Workbook

CHAPTER 25

It's your turn to ride a yak.
Choose to ride bareback or with a saddle.
Draw yourself sitting on the yak's back,
ready to ride.
Print what you say to your friend on the other yak.

_____

Have the students read Polly Parrot's instructions. **Explain:** "Bareback" means no saddle. **Brainstorm** what the students might say to their friend.

Student Workbook

CHAPTER 25 CONTINUED

1. Y

2. y

3. Yak

4. yak

5. Did your yak have a saddle?

6.

7. Do both yaks have saddles?

8. No, both yaks

9. Do yaks eat grass?

10.

Have the students point to and say the letter names and print. They are to read the questions and print the answers. **Note:** They may need help with "don't" in number 8.

Ask: What is the first letter in Yak? (Y is the first letter in yak.)

Ask: How many Yaks have a saddle? (One yak has a saddle.)   **Ask:** Do yaks have horns? (Yes, they do.)

Ask: What is this yak eating? (It's eating grass.)   **Ask:** Do you eat grass? (No, I don't.)

Student Workbook

CHAPTER 26

1. Z

2. z

3. Zebra

4. zebra

5. What is the first letter in  ?

6. The first _____ is

7. Do zebras have stripes?

8. Yes,

Have the children print the letter Zz.

Read question # 5. The children are to complete printing the answer and draw a zebra in the box.

Ask: Do zebras have stripes? (Yes, they do.) (Yes, they have stripes.)

Ask: What color are their stripes? (They are black and white,)

If appropriate: Explain that the sun's shadows make the colors look different or perhaps the young zebra was rolling on the ground.

CHAPTERS 13 TO 26

Some animals are nice to touch.
Draw a picture of an animal you would like to touch.
Write a sentence naming your animal and telling how it would feel.

WORDS TO HELP YOU:

soft   warm   prickly   cold   furry   hard   slippery

Have the students read Polly Parrot's instructions.

They are to look through their books to decide which animal to choose.

Review the word list explaining any that are new. Print pronouns or verbs on the board as needed.

Student Workbook

CHAPTERS 13 TO 26

Find a bird that makes a loud noise.
Draw a picture of the bird.
Write a sentence that tells the bird's name
and the sound it makes.

WORDS TO HELP YOU:
Umbrellabird   makes   BOOOM BOOOM   loud

Have the students read Polly Parrot's instructions.
The students will need to look in their Reader to find the best picture of the umbrellabird.
Review the word list explaining any that are new. Print pronouns or verbs on the board as needed.
Print words on the board as needed.

CHAPTERS 13 TO 26

Find a friendly animal.
Draw a picture of the animal.
Write a sentence that tells the animal's name
and where it lives.

WORDS TO HELP YOU:

ocean   cold   swims   lives

Have the students read Polly Parrot's instructions.
They are to look through their books to decide which animal to choose.
Review the word list explaining any words that are new. Print pronouns or verbs on the board as needed.

Student Workbook

CHAPTERS 13 TO 26

Find a dangerous animal.
Draw a picture of the animal.
Write a sentence that tells the animal's name
and what it eats.

WORDS TO HELP YOU:

Crocodiles   reindeer   eat   snakes   rats

Have the students read Polly Parrot's instructions.

They are to look through their books to decide which animal to choose.

Review the word list explaining any words that are new. Print pronouns or verbs on the board as needed.

Student Workbook

ESL ANIMALS 2
The ALPHABET   M TO Z

Teacher Guide

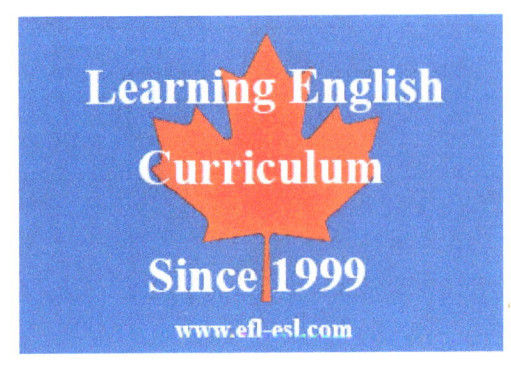

Daisy A. Stocker M.Ed.
George A. Stocker D.D.S.

ESL Animals 2
The Alphabet M TO Z
TEACHER'S GUIDE

CONTENTS		PAGES
Introduction		123
Test 5	Chapters 13 to 16	124 - 127
Test 6	Chapters 17 to 20	128 - 129
Test 7	Chapters 21 to 26	130 - 131
Final Test	Chapters 13 to 26	132 - 135
How to Play Picture Bingo		136
Picture Bingo 5	Review Chapters 11 to 14	137 - 163
Picture Bingo 6	Chapters 15 to 18	164 - 190
Picture Bingo 7	Chapters 19 to 26	191 - 217

TEST 5 CHAPTERS 13 to16 PAGE 1

NAME _____

Exercise 1

Draw a line from each animal to the first letter in its name

m

n

p

o

Exercise 2

Here are 11 porpoises. Draw more to make 16.

Here are 10 seashells. Draw more to make 13.

Have the class point to each animal and say its name. (narwhale, octopus, monkey, porpoises) **Read the instructions for Exercise 1 with them**. Give help with the names of the animals as this test is about listening to the initial sounds, not naming animals. **Note:** Tell the children to do the ones they know first.
Read the instructions for Exercise 2. Before they begin have the children count orally as needed.

TEST 5: CHAPTERS 13 to 16   PAGE 2

NAME _____

Exercise 3:

Draw a line from each paragraph to the picture.

This animal is making a hole
in the shellfish.
It will eat the creature inside

These animals live in the ocean.
They like to jump and play.
They follow boats in the ocean.

These animals live in the cold ocean.
They talk to their friends
with their long tusks.

This animal can jump.
It is sitting in a tree.

Exercise 4:

Do you like animals? _____

Explain: Tell the students that a "paragraph" is a group of sentences that tell about something.
Exercise 3: Have the children point to each picture and name the animals. (porpoises, monkey, octopus, narwhales) They are to read each paragraph and draw a line to the picture it tells about. Review the animal names with them as needed.
Exercise 4: They are to print their answer to the question on the line.

TEST 5: CHAPTERS 13 to16   PAGE 3 ANSWERS

Exercise 1: 5 marks each.

Draw a line from each animal to the first letter in its name.

Exercise 2: 3 marks each.

As directed.

> The test is to identify the children's strengths and weaknesses.
>
> **Encourage them.** Make them feel good about what they know.
>
> **CATCH THEM DOING IT RIGHT!**

Teacher Guide

TEST 5: CHAPTERS 13 to16
ANSWERS CONTINUED

Exercise 3: 6 marks each.
Draw a line from each paragraph to the pictures.

This animal is making a hole
in the shellfish.
It will eat the creature inside

These animals live in the ocean.
They like to jump and play.
They follow boats in the ocean.

These animals live in the cold ocean.
They talk to their friends
with their long tusks.

This animal can jump.
It is sitting in a tree.

Total Marks: 50

Teacher Guide

TEST 6: CHAPTERS 17 to 20 PAGE 1

NAME _____

Draw a line to the first sound in the animal's name.

Qq

Ss

Tt

Rr

Riddles: Choose the animal's name from the box. Print it on the line.

This animal digs in the snow for food.
It has two coats to keep it warm.   _____

The mother lives in the sea.
She lays her eggs in the sand.   _____

This is a very dangerous animal.
It eats deer, crocodiles and snakes.   _____

This is a friendly forest animal.
It goes to sleep in the winter.   _____

| sea turtle | quokka | squirrel | narwhale | tiger | reindeer |

Print your answers in sentences.

Do you eat food?   Yes, I _____

Is it cold in the snow?   Yes, it is _____

128

Teacher Guide

TEST 6: CHAPTERS 17 to 20

ANSWERS Read the instructions with the class for each part of the test. This is a test to assess the children's strengths and difficulties.

It is very important that they understand the instructions.

Sentence answers: Give marks for correct words and word order.

1 Mark each **Note:** Tell the children to do the ones they know first.

Draw a line to the first sound in the animal's name.

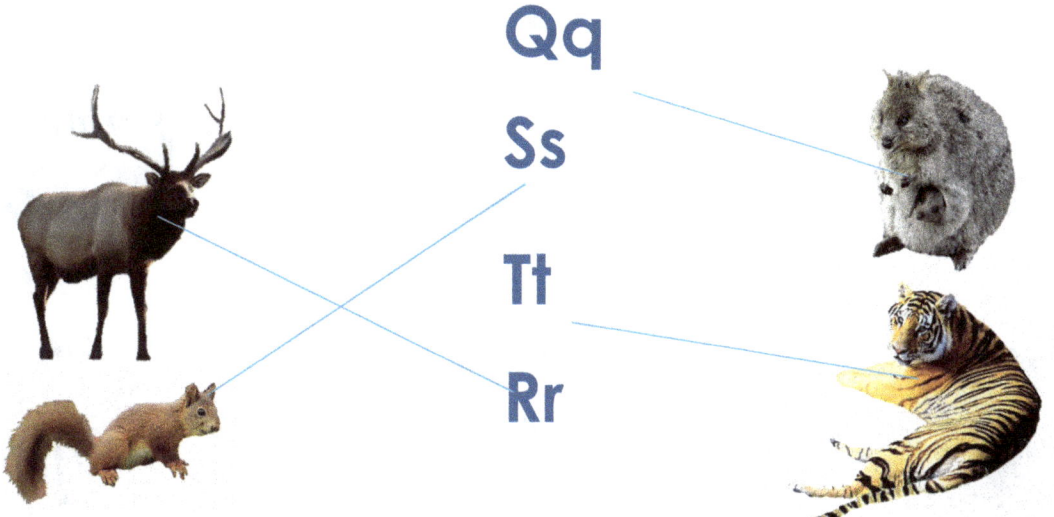

Riddles: Choose the animal's name from the box. Print it on the line.

This animal digs in the snow for food. It has two coats to keep it warm.	*reindeer*
The mother lives in the sea. She lays her eggs in the sand.	*sea turtle*
This is a very dangerous animal. It eats deer, crocodiles and snakes.	*tiger*
This is a friendly forest animal. It goes to sleep in the winter.	*squirrel*

Print your answers in sentences.

Do you eat food?	Yes, I eat food.
Is it cold in the snow?	Yes, it is cold in the snow.

129

Teacher Guide

TEST 7: CHAPTERS 21 to 26   PAGE 1

NAME: _____

Draw a line from the picture to the first letter in its name.

1.

Z z
X x
W w
Y y
U u
V v

2.

3.

4.

5.

6.

Guess these riddles. Choose your answers from the box.
Print your answer on the lines.

7. These birds are scavengers.
   They keep the land clean.   _____

8. This animal lives live on the snow
   and in the cold Arctic waters.   _____

9. This animal has stripes. It looks like a horse.   _____

10. These animals have long hair and big horns.   _____

| Western gorilla | zebra | walrus | umbrellabird | yaks | vultures |

Teacher Guide

CHAPTERS 21 to 26   **TEST 7 ANSWERS**

Draw a line from the picture to the first letter in its name.

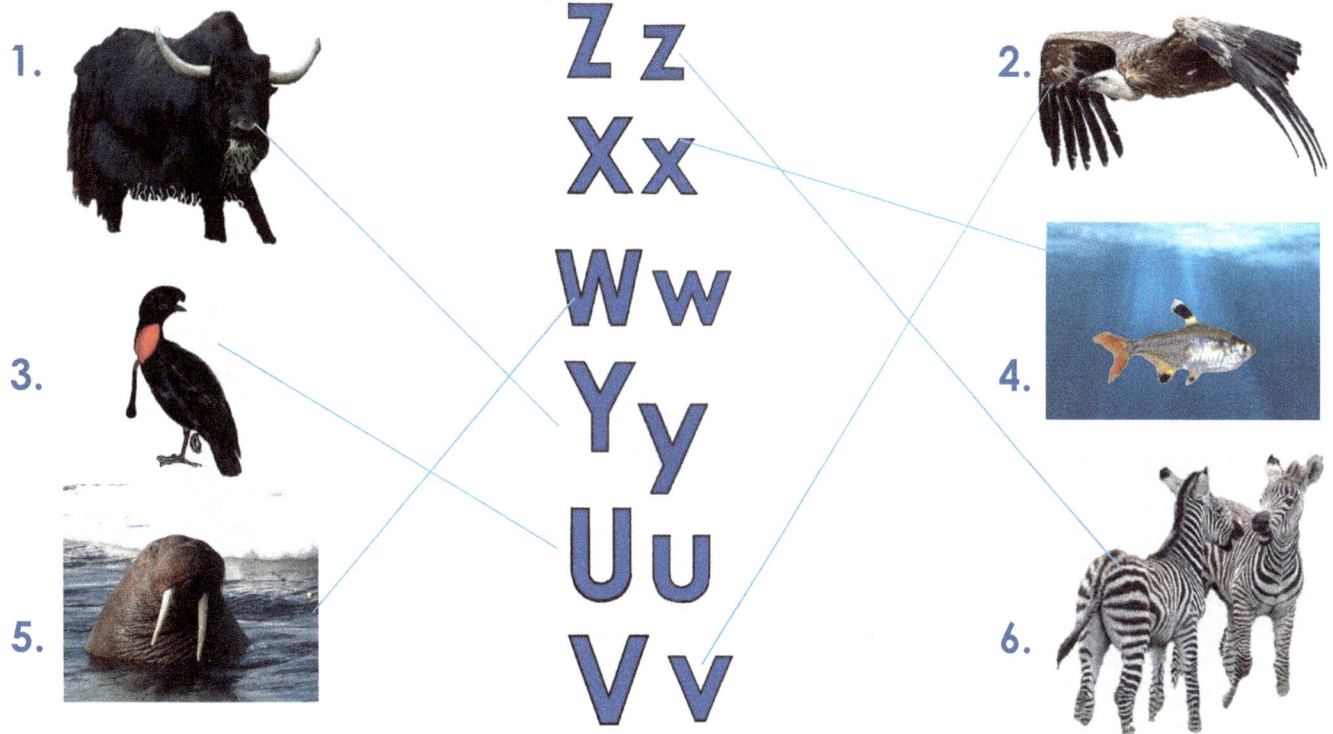

**Guess these riddles. Choose your answers from the box.
Print your answer on the lines.**

7. These birds are scavengers.
   They keep the land clean.   vultures

8. This animal lives live on the snow
   and in the cold Arctic waters.   walrus

9. This animal has stripes. It looks like a horse.   zebra

10. These animals have long hair and big horns.   yaks

> **Read the instructions** to the class and have them say the names of the animals.
> **Review** the names as they work as the test is about listening for the sounds rather than knowing the animals.
> **Total Marks: 10.** One for each correct answer.
> **Note:** Tell the children to do the ones they know first.

Teacher Guide

CHAPTERS 13 to 26   FINAL TEST

NAME _____

Draw a line from the picture to the first letter in its name.

1.    Nn   2.

                          Yy

3.    Tt   4.

                          Qq

5.    Rr   6.

                          Mm

7.    Zz   8.

                          Oo

9.    Ss   10.

                          Pp

11. Is the squirrel in a tree?

12. Yes,

CHAPTERS 13 to 26   FINAL TEST:

NAME _____

Draw a line from the paragraph to the picture.

13. The monkeys are in school.
    They have a monkey teacher.

14. This sea creature is smart.
    It can open a jar.

15. These sea creatures are friendly.
    They like to follow boats
    and jump out of the water.

16. This animal is in the hot jungle.
    It is dangerous!

17. It is winter.
    These animals dig in the snow for food.

CHAPTERS 13 to 26 TEST ANSWERS

Marking Instructions: Read the instructions to the class and have them say the names of the animals. **Review** the names as they work as the test is about listening for the sounds rather than knowing the names. Numbers 1 to 10 (1 mark each) Number 11 (0 marks), Number 12 (5 marks), Numbers 13-17 (2 marks each)
Total Marks: 25. **Note:** Tell the children to do the ones they know first.

1.  → Qq
2. → Mm
3. → Rr
4. → Yy
5. → Pp
6. → Nn
7. → Zz
8. → Ss
9. → Tt
10. → Oo

11. Is the squirrel in a tree?

12. Yes, the squirrel is in a tree.

CHAPTERS 13 to 26 TEST ANSWERS

The monkeys are in school.
They have a monkey teacher.

This sea creature is smart.
It can open a jar.

These sea creatures are friendly.
They like to follow boats
and jump out of the water.

This animal is in the hot jungle.
It is dangerous!

It is winter.
These animals dig in the snow for food.

TEACHER'S GUIDE
CHAPTERS 13 to 26

HOW TO PLAY PICTURE BINGO

Give each student one Bingo Card. For classes with more than 25 students, two or three students can have copies of the same card. It's best if those with identical cards are sitting apart.
The teacher calls the captions listed below in any order. The children are to mark the picture that matches the caption. We suggest that the students use a small object such as a bean or a chestnut.

When they have a horizontal, vertical or diagonal row of pictures with an object in each box, they are to call **BINGO**. The diagonal row must go from corner to corner. The central BINGO box is free.

It is important that the children be allowed to help each other or be given teacher assistance. They should all find the correct picture to match the caption that is called. After playing two or three games they should be encouraged to work independently, although some children will need extra help.
NOTE: The teacher will need to mark the captions as he or she calls and check for mistakes on the papers of the winners

Play calling the Teacher's Captions for many games until the children understand and play without difficulty.

The children use the same cards for the Enrichment Captions. They will learn to use context clues to understand the new words. Play many times.

Student Card sample.

PRIZES: The winners will be delighted with a star or a rubberstamp picture drawn on their exercise book. The same BINGO card can be used for many games by using beans or other small objects. (Dry pasta is good.) Tell the children to keep their cards clean, without marks, so they can play many games. These games motivate the children to learn by listening, understanding and associating the meaning to the picture. They are also learning basic grammar without any formal teaching.
NOTE: The children will be ready for Picture Bingo when they finish Chapter 14.

BINGO 5　　　　　　　　　　　　TEACHER'S COPY

137

BINGO 5   ENRICHMENT COPY

Bingo

138

CHAPTERS 11 to 14   BINGO 5   CARD 1

Bingo

CHAPTERS 11 to 14 BINGO 5 CARD 2

140

CHAPTERS 11 to 14   BINGO 5   CARD 3

141

Bingo

CHAPTERS 11 to 14   **BINGO 5**   **CARD 4**

Bingo

CHAPTERS 11 to 14   BINGO 5   CARD 5

Bingo

CHAPTERS 11 to 14   BINGO 5   CARD 6

Bingo

CHAPTERS 11 to 14　　BINGO 5　　CARD 7

145

Bingo

CHAPTERS 11 to 14 BINGO 5 CARD 8

Bingo

CHAPTERS 11 to 14   BINGO 5   CARD 9

CHAPTERS 11 to 14   BINGO 5   CARD 10

Bingo

CHAPTERS 11 to 14   BINGO 5   CARD 11

Bingo

CHAPTERS 11 to 14 BINGO 5 CARD 12

CHAPTERS 11 to 14 **BINGO 5** **CARD 14**

Bingo

CHAPTERS 11 to 14   BINGO 5   CARD 15

Bingo

153

CHAPTERS 11 to 14   BINGO 5   CARD 16

Bingo

154

CHAPTERS 11 to 14   **BINGO 5**   **CARD 17**

Bingo

CHAPTERS 11 to 14 **BINGO 5** **CARD 18**

Bingo

CHAPTERS 11 to 14 **BINGO 5** **CARD 19**

Bingo

CHAPTERS 11 to 14 **BINGO 5** **CARD 20**

Bingo

CHAPTERS 11 to 14   **BINGO 5**   **CARD 21**

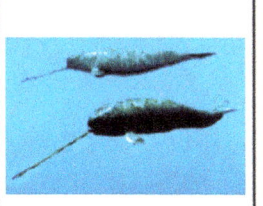	**M**	 **O**	**O**	
	**k**		**K**	
		**BINGO**		
n		**m**	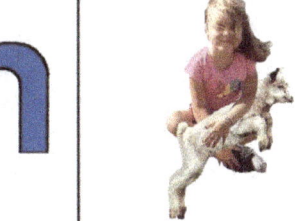	**L**
			**N**	

Bingo

CHAPTERS 11 to 14 BINGO 5 CARD 22

Bingo

CHAPTERS 11 to 14   BINGO 5   CARD 23

Bingo

CHAPTERS 11 to 14 **BINGO 5** **CARD 24**

162

Bingo

CHAPTERS 11 to 14 BINGO 5 CARD 25

Bingo

CHAPTERS 15 to 18 **BINGO 6** **TEACHER'S COPY**

164

Bingo

CHAPTERS 15 to 18　　BINGO 6　　ENRICHMENT

165

CHAPTERS 15 to 18   BINGO 6   CARD 1

Bingo

CHAPTERS 15 to 18   BINGO 6   CARD 2

167
Bingo

CHAPTERS 15 to 18 BINGO 6 CARD 3

Bingo

CHAPTERS 15 to 18 **BINGO 6** **CARD 4**

Bingo

CHAPTERS 15 to 18 **BINGO 6** **CARD 5**

170

Bingo

CHAPTERS 15 to 18   BINGO 6   CARD 6

Bingo

CHAPTERS 15 to 18 BINGO 6 CARD 7

CHAPTERS 15 to 18   BINGO 6   CARD 8

CHAPTERS 15 to 18 **BINGO 6** **CARD 9**

Bingo

CHAPTERS 15 to 18 **BINGO 6** **CARD 10**

Bingo

CHAPTERS 15 to 18 **BINGO 6** **CARD 11**

Bingo

CHAPTERS 15 to 18 BINGO 6 CARD 12

Bingo

CHAPTERS 15 to 18 **BINGO 6** **CARD 13**

CHAPTERS 15 to 18 BINGO 6 CARD 14

Bingo

CHAPTERS 15 to 18   BINGO 6   CARD 15

Bingo

CHAPTERS 15 to 18   BINGO 6   CARD 16

Bingo

CHAPTERS 15 to 18   BINGO 6   CARD 17

Bingo

CHAPTERS 15 to 18 **BINGO 6** **CARD 18**

Bingo

CHAPTERS 15 to 18   BINGO 6   CARD 19

Bingo

CHAPTERS 15 to 18   BINGO 6   CARD 20

Bingo

CHAPTERS 15 to 18   BINGO 6   CARD 21

186

Bingo

CHAPTERS 15 to 18 **BINGO 6** **CARD 22**

CHAPTERS 15 to 18　　　BINGO 6　　　CARD 23

188

Bingo

CHAPTERS 15 to 18 BINGO 6 CARD 24

189

CHAPTERS 15 to 18 **BINGO 6** **CARD 25**

Bingo

CHAPTERS 19 to 26 — BINGO 7 — Teacher's Copy

U u		V v		
This is the first letter in umbrellabird.	The squirrel is sitting on a branch.	This is capital V and small v.	The x-ray Tetra swims in warm rivers.	The umbrellabird calls BOOOM BOOOM!
	S s			
The yak's long hair keeps it warm.	This is the first letter in squirrel.	It's an umbrella.	It's tropical trees and water	George is wearing a red shirt.
		BINGO		T t
It's a brown rabbit.	There is snow on the ground.		Z is the first letter in this animal's name.	This is the first letter in tiger.
		X x		Y y
The sea turtle is in the ocean.	The gorilla is very big and strong.	This is the first letter in x-ray tetra.	The tiger has a cub.	This is the letter Y.
W w			Z z	
This is the first letter in walrus.	This huge bird eats dead animals.	The walrus lives in the cold Arctic.	This is the first letter in zoo.	You can see inside this animals mouth.

Bingo

CHAPTERS 19 to 26   BINGO 7   Enrichment Copy

Uu This is capital U and small u.	 This animal has a beautiful big tail.	Vv It is the first letter in vulture.	 It's an x-ray Tetra.	 This bird calls BOOOM in the tropical jungle.
 This animal has a saddle on its back.	Ss This is the first letter in snake.	 You need this when it rains	 It's a tropical jungle by a pond.	 George is sitting on the yak.
 This brown animal has very long ears.	 It's cold and snowy.	BINGO	 This animal has black and white stripes.	Tt It is capital T and small t.
 This turtle has a shell on its back.	 The gorilla lives in the hot jungle.	Xx This is capital X and small x.	 The two animals have orange and black stripes.	Yy This is the first letter in yak.
Ww This is the first letter in water.	 This bird is a scavenger.	 This animal has huge tusks	Zz This is the letter Z.	 You can see this animal's sharp teeth.

Bingo

CHAPTERS 19 to 26 — **BINGO 7** — **CARD 1**

Uu		Vv		
	Ss			
		BINGO		Tt
		Xx		Yy
Ww			Zz	

Bingo

CHAPTERS 19 to 26   **BINGO 7**   **CARD 2**

Y y		S s		
	U u			
		BINGO	V v	T t
	W w	X x		
			Z z	

Bingo

CHAPTERS 19 to 26 BINGO 7 CARD 3

Bingo

CHAPTERS 19 to 26 BINGO 7 CARD 4

Bingo

CHAPTERS 19 to 26 BINGO 7 CARD 5

Bingo

CHAPTERS 19 to 26　　　BINGO 7　　　CARD 6

U u		V v		
	W w			
		BINGO	S s	T t
	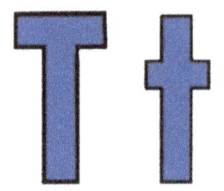	X x		Y y
			Z z	

Bingo

CHAPTERS 19 to 26   BINGO 7   CARD 7

U u		X x		
	S s			
T t	V v	BINGO		
				Y y
W w			Z z	

Bingo

CHAPTERS 19 to 26 **BINGO 7** **CARD 8**

Bingo

CHAPTERS 19 to 26 BINGO 7 CARD 9

Bingo

CHAPTERS 19 to 26 BINGO 7 CARD 10

Bingo

CHAPTERS 19 to 26 BINGO 7 CARD 11

Bingo

CHAPTERS 19 to 26 **BINGO 7** **CARD 12**

204

Bingo

CHAPTERS 19 to 26   **BINGO 7**   **CARD 13**

Bingo

CHAPTERS 19 to 26   BINGO 7   CARD 14

Bingo

CHAPTERS 19 to 26 BINGO 7 CARD 15

Bingo

CHAPTERS 19 to 26   **BINGO 7**   **CARD 16**

	Vv			Yy
			Ww	Zz
		BINGO		
Tt	Ss	Uu		
		Xx		

Bingo

CHAPTERS 19 to 26 **BINGO 7** **CARD 17**

Bingo

CHAPTERS 19 to 26 **BINGO 7** **CARD 18**

Ww	Vv			
Yy			Ss	Zz
		BINGO		
	Xx	Uu		
	Tt			

Bingo

CHAPTERS 19 to 26   **BINGO 7**   **CARD 19**

Bingo

CHAPTERS 19 to 26　　　BINGO 7　　　CARD 20

Bingo

CHAPTERS 19 to 26 BINGO 7 CARD 21

Bingo

CHAPTERS 19 to 26   **BINGO 7**   **CARD 23**

Tt				
Zz				
Uu	Xx	BINGO		Ww
	Yy			Ss
	Vv			

Bingo

CHAPTERS 19 to 26 **BINGO 7** **CARD 24**

	**Uu**			
Zz	**Yy**			
	**Xx**	BINGO		**Ww**
	**Tt**			**Ss**
	**Vv**			

Bingo

CHAPTERS 19 to 26   BINGO 7   CARD 25

Bingo

217

www.ingramcontent.com/pod-product-compliance
Lightning Source LLC
Chambersburg PA
CBHW080342170426
43194CB00014B/2655